Introduction

You've heard the whine of the powerful motors as the cars scream down a straightaway. You've seen the dirt fly as they tear into a hairpin curve. You've seen the checkered flag drop as one car flashes across the finish line a split second ahead of the others!

Now you want to experience it for yourself— the awesome thrills of radio controlled racing cars!

This book is a great place to start. It will tell you everything you need to know to get started in one of the fastest-growing sports around. You'll learn about how the cars work. You'll find out which questions to ask when the time comes to buy your first RC car. And you'll get lots of great tips on painting and decorating your car, on how to practice driving, on driving safety, and on how to find an RC car club.

With this book as your guide, you'll definitely get started the right way. And remember that RC cars have become one of the hottest hobbies around—they're a whole lot of fun. Competition racing is a great way to experience the thrill of RC cars. But don't forget that you can have a blast just driving around at the school yard or on your own driveway.

So, get ready. The fun is about to begin!

THE WINNER'S GUIDE TO

RADIO CONTROLLED CAR RACING

by C.M. Gynn

Thanks to Kim Rossey, Ohio Division Director of NORRCA (National Organization for Racing Radio Controlled Autos), for his patient help, and to all the racers at Action Hobby and Raceway, Columbus, Ohio. Special thanks to Robby Nicholson, a great young racer, and to his mom, Marie, his biggest fan.

Special thanks to Mike Nicholas of Nicholas Mini-Baja Raceway, 1405 E. Main Street, Columbus, Ohio 43205, where the cover photo was taken.

Published by Willowisp Press, Inc.
401 E. Wilson Bridge Road, Worthington, Ohio 43085

Printed in the United States of America

10 9 8 7 6 5 4 3 2 1

ISBN   0-87406-417-1

Table of Contents

Let's Meet Your RC Race Car

Take a look at a radio controlled car. Check out the slick paint job and the decals. It looks just like a full-size racer—great in every way. Each car is different, just like all people are different. And just like people, some cars can be faster and stronger. But every car has the same basic parts. Let's learn about some of these important parts.

Take a Closer Look

You can understand the insides of a car easily if you think of them in terms of the human body. What part can you compare the heart to? That's easy. The heart works like the motor of the car. What can you compare the brain to? There are three parts in a radio controlled car that make up the "thinking" parts. These thinking parts work together to send messages—the transmit-

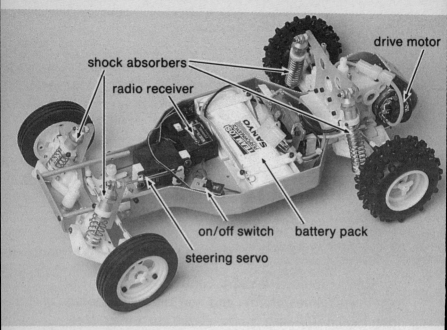

The parts of an RC car.

ter talks to the receiver and the servos. What can the skeleton be compared to? The skeleton is like the chassis (rhymes with Lassie). It's the frame that supports the working parts.

How about the veins and arteries? Instead of carrying blood, the wiring carries electricity. Food is energy for a person, but in the RC car it's the battery pack that provides the juice. An athlete training for the big game will be sure to eat right to have the most energy. Your car's battery pack needs to be charged correctly for prime performance, too.

That leaves the body. Well, that one's too easy. You can figure it out for yourself!

Magic or Science?

Even though you know what all these parts do, RC racing still may seem like magic. A car obeys your every command, even when you're standing 50 feet away. But it's not magic. It's science.

The hand-held transmitter—sort of like a joy stick on a video game—sends radio signals to the receiver in the RC car. The receiver talks to motorized servos, which control the direction and speed of the car. Your car receives the signal from your transmitter only.

You know you can change your radio dial to different stations to hear different music. It's pretty much the same thing with radio controlled cars. You have to tune your transmitter and receiver to the same "station" with the use of radio crystals. That's called the frequency.

If your car responded to other transmitters, there would be smash ups everywhere at the races. That's why you'll find extra crystals for sale. An extra set of crystals changes the frequency your car runs on. If you take part in a race, you'll have to register your frequency with the race officials. Any duplicate frequencies can't be in the same race.

That's why it's important when you buy your equipment that you get a transmitter that has changeable crystals. This way, you'll have a spare set of crystals just in case someone else on your block or at a race has the same frequency as yours. Switching crystals is easy. And you can always ask around for help. Learning from others is part of any great hobby or sport. Drivers of radio controlled cars are always happy to help out beginners.

What Makes Your RC Car Run?

Electric Motors in Your RC Car

Radio controlled cars have electric motors that run on battery packs. You can get gas engines in the larger styles, but most hobby stores feature the electric, battery-powered systems.

Battery packs are usually six sub-C cell batteries in a plastic wrap. That's six batteries a little smaller than a flashlight battery, all packaged together. You take the pack out of the car after each use and recharge it with a battery charger.

Just like with full-size cars, the fuel is used up faster by cars that have more under the hood. The family car burns a lot less gasoline than an engine meant for racing. But then again, the car meant for racing won't go as far as the family buggy without making a pit stop. Battery packs for the RC cars are all the same.

If you are just driving around without a lot of extras on your car, you can expect about 20 to 30 minutes of driving time per battery charge. If you put those extras in, you may be lucky to get the four minutes needed to complete an official race!

After draining the juice from the battery pack, you have to recharge the pack using the battery charger. The battery charger plugs into an outlet like any other electrical appliance. The battery packs are made to be recharged, not thrown out, after each use. In other words, don't think that you can get away with not buying a battery charger. The charger is an important part of your RC system. You need to give the motor the electricity it needs, and a charger for your battery pack is the only way to do it. So, buy a battery charger when you buy your RC car. It isn't a luxury. It's a necessity.

There are several other kinds of battery chargers that can be used where you don't have access to an electrical outlet. At some outdoor races, the sponsors provide juice from a series of car (full-size) batteries wired together. Unless you're going to be running your car far away from civilization (that is, away from an electrical outlet) you won't need to set up a portable energy source.

Here's a word of caution about this electrical business. Remember that you're dealing with a powerful energy source. Make sure you warn your little brothers and sisters about not messing around with the battery charger. If you have any questions, ask an adult.

Let's Get Technical

There are kits available for building your own motor from parts. But the motor is usually provided assembled and ready for installation. If you do build your own motor, you'll learn a lot about electricity. And you'll be miles ahead of the other kids in science class when you study electricity!

But even if you don't build your own motor, you should have a basic understanding of how an electric motor is put together. This way, if your car ever breaks down at a race, you can at least check out the parts that you are familiar with. Your car will be only as fast as its motor allows it to be. By understanding the motor, you can understand how to make it give more power to the car.

Inside the motor casing, you'll find the rotor. What's that, you ask? Well, you're about to learn some Latin. Think of the word rotate. That means to turn, which is what the rotor does. Its Latin root word is *rota*, which means wheel. (Try that on your parents if they say this car stuff isn't educational!)

The rotor turns because the electrical current from the batteries causes the rotor to become a magnet. As a magnet, it goes toward other mag-

RC monster truck in action.

nets. The rotor goes toward the field magnets that are also part of the motor case.

This type of motor is called a DC, or direct current, motor. The electrical current comes directly from the energy source, the battery pack. The current goes from the battery pack into soft brushes. Then it is fed into the wire that is wrapped around an arm that sticks out from the rotor.

You start with energy in the battery pack. You want it to go into the brushes and then travel to the wire wound around the arm of the rotor. To get the most energy to the rotor, you have to be sure the electric current is traveling on the most direct path. You don't want it to be sidetracked or slowed down by resistance.

Break It In the Right Way

There are some simple things you can do to make sure your motor is receiving power correctly. First, before you put a new motor in your RC car, put the motor up on a block. Then hook it to the battery pack. Run the motor slowly to give all the parts time to settle in. Recharge the batteries, and then let it run some more. This is to let the brushes form themselves to the right curve so that you have the most brush contact as possible with the power source.

If you have a car that is assembled when you buy it, you can accomplish the same result by putting the car up on a block to keep the tires off the ground. Then run the car slowly for two or three battery charges.

This way you're not asking the motor to do much work while it's being broken in. If you take a couple of hours at the beginning to break in your motor the right way, you'll get longer life and faster speeds later.

Motor Maintenance in Minutes

Once you've gone to all the trouble of making sure your motor is broken in properly, set aside a few minutes after each run to keep the motor in top shape.

If you don't have a small compressor that sprays pressurized air (the kind that is used for air-brush painting is ideal), get a can of pressurized air from a hobby or camera shop. It looks just like a spray-paint can, but it contains only clean air. It comes with a straw to attach to the nozzle so you can direct little bursts of air into tight spaces and clean them completely.

After each run, take the car body off. Using the nozzle straw of the canned air, spray out any dust and dirt that may have settled on the motor or servos. The dirt comes off easily if you don't let it build up. And remember that a clean machine will run faster and longer!

Buying Your RC Car

Before Mom and Dad buy a car, they test-drive it. They wouldn't think of buying the family wheels without first taking a model for a spin.

Take a Test-talk

Test-driving a radio controlled car is going to be harder than just walking into a car dealership and having the salesperson give you the keys to the car. Don't blame friends for not letting you drive their car, either. An RC car is a pretty big investment to lend out. You can, however, make an intelligent choice by "test-talking" a car.

Even though most places won't let you take a car out of the box and drive it around, you can learn a lot about the model by watching and asking questions. A salesperson at your local hobby shop will probably be able to tell you about several different cars.

You might even want to take your favorite adult

with you. For one thing, you might need someone to drive you there. Plus the more involved your adult gets with radio controlled cars, the better. This will be helpful when you need a ride to practice or a race. Best of all, when the adult sees how much fun RC racing is, he or she might want to pitch in and help you get a car!

Find a Club or a Track

Another way to learn about RC cars is to find out where a radio controlled car club holds its races and practices. This is the place to really talk cars with the serious racers.

How do you find an RC car club? Check the

Watch the dirt fly!

phone book. In the yellow pages, you can look up "hobby shops." Call each one, and ask if they know where a radio controlled car club meets. If they aren't sure, ask if there is one particular salesperson who is the radio controlled racing expert. Even if the store doesn't know about a club, the individual person might. Or, try calling your local newspaper sports editor. The newspaper might have done a story on the opening of a radio controlled racetrack in your area. And that might lead to information about a club.

If you find a track, that's great. But don't give up if there isn't one in your area. With the way this sport is growing, your area is probably going to get one soon. Keep checking. You don't have to wait for a racetrack to come to your city before you get your car, but it is fun to see a race. Maybe you could ask your parents about going to a race in another city. You could make it a family affair.

Everybody Was a Beginner Once!

At your hobby shop or at the RC car club practice, you'll find lots of people who will be happy to give you advice on your first car. Remember, even the racer who takes the checkered flag was a rookie once. People want to see others have a good time with radio controlled racing. That's the way the sport grows.

Ask questions. Ask more questions. You'll hear arguments for getting one model over another from one person, and then you'll hear the exact opposite from another driver. Everyone has a favorite car.

Why is there so much confusion about which RC car model is the best? Some people like Chevies, and some like Fords, don't they? Different models have different characteristics that one driver will favor over the characteristics of another type of car. Drivers want a car that will give their driving style an edge over the other cars in a race. Even if you drive just for fun by yourself, you still want a car that gives you the best handling for your skill level.

You and your car make a team. You don't have to buy the most expensive model in the store to get started. You can get a reliable car for a reasonable price. Taking care of your investment will pay off in two ways. You'll learn about RC cars in general, and you'll show that you're responsible enough to upgrade your car as your skill improves.

What You Need
to Know

One of the biggest choices you'll have to make is "Do I buy, or do I build?" Here's some information to help you decide.

Buying or Building?

Strength and durability are key features to look for in your radio controlled car. Racing around the neighborhood or around the track, RC cars have to be amazingly tough to withstand the incredible beating. No ready-to-run RC car or kit is going to advertise that it's weak and breakable. How, then, are you going to pick one that has what it takes to stand up to your workouts or a race?

One way is to purchase a lower-priced model now, and then soup it up with modifications later. As your skill improves, you can improve your car. If this approach is for you, be sure that the car you select can be modified. Unfortunately, ready-made stock models, which are the most inexpensive RC cars, usually can't be modified.

The best advice is to buy as much car as your budget allows, even if that means waiting a month or two to save the money. If you are relying on the favorite adults in your life to buy the car for you, then it is up to you to educate them on the features they should look for in a desirable radio controlled car kit.

It is not easy to convince someone to spend twice as much for a kit you have to put together than for an off-the-shelf, assembled model. In fact, buying a kit may not be the way for you to go at all. If you're not sure about your interest in the sport, you might want to try a less expensive model to start. You can still have lots of fun with it. But the drawback is that when it breaks, you'll be pretty well stuck with a broken car and little hope of fixing it.

Another way to start is to buy a used car that someone else built from scratch. That way, you'll probably be able to upgrade the car later. Look in the local papers, and check with the RC clubs for a good buy. Be cautious with this, though. Have the car checked out by an expert from the local club before buying it. You can find plenty of honest bargains from people who are trading up in the field, but you could get a real lemon, too. It's just like in the full-size car business—don't buy it before having it checked out.

Features to Look For
No matter what type or brand of RC car you buy,

there are certain features that will help you drive the car fast and accurately. There are controls that will be more sensitive to the signals so the car will follow your every command. More importantly for the beginner, some parts of the car need to be stronger when the car doesn't follow your every command and goes full speed into a wall! (It will happen. Just don't try to test it that way on purpose.) To select your basic car, use the information you gathered in talking to the folks at the hobby shop. Check the features against that list.

The Suspension

The suspension is the link between the car and

The drive train of an RC car.

tires. It supports the upper part of the car on the wheel axles. The suspension is almost alive, reacting to each bump the ground has to offer and pushing the tires against the racing surface. If the suspension doesn't respond, the tires will lose contact with the ground. They'll be twirling in the stratosphere doing absolutely nothing. You lose speed, and you lose control. If you want precise control and prime speed, and you want to beat yourself or your competitors, don't ignore the suspension.

Ask about the front and rear suspension. Look for the heavy-duty, metal ball linkage suspension. You'll find that kits and cars offer both plastic suspension pieces and heavier metal ones. The plastic pieces tend to catch on themselves. The heavier metal ones move more precisely.

The heavy-duty suspension can be adjusted more easily, too. You want to be able to tighten the suspension to an absolute dead-drop. That means when you set the car on the ground and lift up the rear end and drop it from the height of about four inches, the car just thuds. It doesn't bounce back up at all.

This makes real sense when you think about the dynamics of driving. When the car goes over a bump, the tires go into the air. Not touching the ground, the tires just spin. When the tires hit the ground again, you want them to stay there, not bounce back up and waste more time in the air. So, a dead-drop suspension is the adjustment you want. If your suspension system can't deliver that, you're going to be in for less than optimum driving.

Adjustable, four-wheel independent suspension is another alternative that will let you make changes in your car for different driving surfaces. The same rules apply, though, as for the dead-drop suspension. You want to keep the wheels in contact with the ground as much as possible.

Buzz Words You'll Want to Know

There are a few buzz words that will help you sound like you know what you're talking about when you discuss the suspension system with the hobby shop salesperson. And you'll understand what the salesperson says about why these things are important.

The *Camber* is the leaning angle of the wheels. If the tires lean out with the bottoms closer together than the tops, that's positive camber. That's what you want for better driving control.

The *Caster* is the placement of the ball joints on the wheels. When the top ball joint of the wheel is behind the bottom ball joint, that's called positive caster. This means the wheels will lean to the rear of the car. This arrangement gives you greater steering stability.

Toe-in and toe-out is the placement of the wheels closer together at their front than at their back, and the other way around. Point your toes toward each other, and look at your heels. Your toes are closer together than your heels. That's toe-in. Point your toes away from each other, and look at your heels. Your toes are farther apart now. That's toe-out.

Travel is the return motion of the suspension

system. How much can the suspension system "travel" when it hits a big bump?

The camber, caster, toe-in, and travel should all be easily adjustable so that you can adapt your car to different surfaces. By adjusting the camber, you can give the tires more bite as you drive around corners. Camber adjustment assures proper tire contact with the ground. You can start at a 45 degree angle when you first set up and make adjustments from there. For straightaway drag racing, you won't need to worry about camber as much as you will for a snake course. You'll want to adjust the camber to a steeper angle if you are faced with hairpin turns.

The caster is important for the steering stability. If your car isn't responding to the steering commands, then you should look at the tire placement. Start by setting the wheels according to the car's direction, and give yourself time to become familiar with driving. If you want more response, put the wheels a bit more to the back of the ball joint.

The front wheels of your car should be adjusted for toe-in, and the rear wheels should be adjusted for toe-out. This is the best arrangement for most surfaces.

Travel is what allows the suspension to soak up the surprise of a headfirst dive into the dirt after a jump. You want the system with the most travel if you ever plan to do much jumping. If your car does a nosedive with any speed, the suspension system needs to be able to cushion that shock.

The mechanics of radio controlled cars are really the same as for full-size cars. Basically, these are the things that the garage mechanic checks when your family car gets an alignment. If your parents' car couldn't be aligned, it wouldn't be around long.

You'll be able to align a good RC car, too. If the car doesn't have adjustable features, that doesn't mean it doesn't need adjustments. It just means you won't be able to do it yourself. The cars without adjustable features won't last as long, either. They'll probably be just fine for a few really good jumps. It's landing that will do them in.

The Transmission

The transmission is made up of the parts, including the speed-changing gears and the propeller shaft, that transmit power from the motor to the drive shaft. The transmission better do its job, or your car won't be going very far or very fast for very long!

The drive shaft is connected to the differential, and together the transmission and drive shaft are called the power train. The differential is the set of gears that makes it possible for the rear wheels to turn at different speeds. If your car turns a corner, the inside wheel turns slower than the outside wheel. If it didn't, you would not be able to turn the car. This isn't just radio controlled car driving. These scientific principles apply to full-size automobiles as well.

For the dirt-burners, you are going to need a transmission that delivers lots of torque so the car can blast out of holes. Torque is a force that produces rotation. The motor must deliver torque to the drive shaft to spin the wheels.

The Body
Most RC car bodies are made of plastic, and a few are made of fiberglass. A brand of plastic called Lexan is about as tough as plastic gets. Look for it. Using the Lexan body will protect your hard work on the car so it won't be cracked or chipped the first time you hit a wall.

The Chassis
Look for a tempered aluminum chassis in a tub design. A plastic or fiberglass chassis just doesn't seem to hold. A tubular design isn't going to protect the sensitive radio equipment as well as a full tub, either.

Ground Clearance Specs
The uneven conditions of dirt courses means ground clearance is very important. If you are always going to drive on a flat, oval track, ground clearance can be next to nothing. For the soil-slammers, though, the car should sit high, at or above the half-way mark of the back tires.

Some other points to consider in your list of features when buying an RC car include a low center of gravity to keep the car stable on turns, motor placement over the drive wheels for better traction, modular wheels that can be replaced for different driving conditions, and rollover protection so the whole car doesn't self-destruct when you roll it.

Each expert racer has a different favorite brand

name car. Sometimes when the experts endorse one product over another, it's not so much because one brand is better. Rather, it can be that one manufacturer pays more money to the expert than another company.

All the claims and counter-claims can confuse a guy. But don't let that bother you. Let your own knowledge work for you. The growth of radio controlled cars brings new manufacturers to the market each season. What is hot this week may not be hot next month.

Use your best judgment. Weigh cost against features, and look for the best balance. Get your car, and let's go!

Size, Style, Speed, and Safety

RC cars are modeled after full-size cars and trucks. There are as many different RC car models as there are road cars. Most RC cars are modeled after hot stock cars, Indy cars, or formula racers. And don't forget RC monster trucks, which are as awesome as the real thing.

What Size to Get?

RC cars are available in five different sizes. Electric cars are available in 1/8, 1/10, 1/12, and 1/24 sizes. Gas cars come in 1/4 and 1/8 sizes.

The 1/24 is small, small, small. A Ferrari only measures five inches, bumper to bumper. The price sometimes is smaller, too, but not always. You'll have an easy time taking this back and forth to your racing spot—whether it's the school parking lot or a racetrack. If you plan to go to

A 1/10 size RC car.

the track, though, you may have trouble finding other cars this size to race.

The 1/10 is probably the most common size. A model of a 15-foot dune buggy is going to be about a foot and a half long. It's big enough to work with, but small enough to store and carry to the track.

The 1/12 and 1/8 sizes are not quite as popular as the 1/10. If you go with the 1/10, you'll have the most options in racing, upgrading, and availability. You'll have a wider choice of decals, too.

Don't Forget the Gas Guzzlers

RC cars with gasoline engines come in sizes of 1/4 and 1/8, which are about three to five feet long. Gas cars are available in other sizes, too, but they are not very common. The gas engine is a bit more expensive, and it's more dangerous because gas is flammable. Before battery-powered electric RC cars were widely available, gas models were the only racers. There are still some very big races for gas cars throughout the country. One racer who converted to electric says the only thing he misses about the gas racing are the fiery crashes. And he only misses those when it wasn't his car!

Actually, technology has improved in gas engines as well, making them safer than they were a few decades ago. There is still a dedicated group of gas modelers out there. If you're lucky enough to know one, you can learn a lot about engines, cars, and racing. This book concentrates on the electric cars.

Speeds and Surfaces

RC cars are made to run either on dirt or on a smooth surface like concrete, blacktop, or carpet. If the car can run on dirt, it's called an off-road vehicle. You can, of course, run an off-road car on a track. But a car made just for smoother track racing shouldn't be run on dirt.

Thirty-five miles per hour is a common speed for off-road RC racing cars driven by expert drivers. With a stock, off-the-shelf RC car model, you won't have any trouble speeding along at 18 to 20 miles per hour. That's one fast bundle of wires and wheels, and one dangerous one if you aren't careful and don't watch the car closely.

RC Safety Common Sense

You don't need a driver's license to operate a radio controlled car, but there are some safety rules you need to know. You've probably taken a bicycle safety course. Those rules work here, too. Remember to watch out for the other guy, and don't play in traffic.

Here are a few safety pointers.

Beware of pedestrians. If people are walking near where you are driving, make sure they see your car. After all, how many times has Dad tripped over the dog? Don't let him trip over your car. He won't like it. You won't like it. And your car certainly won't like it. The dog might not care, but that's another story.

Beware of babies. Babies are, well, they're babies. Unlike adults, babies can see little moving objects very well. They just don't know what to do with them if they catch them. Eating them is one thing they might do, which is not a very good idea for your car or for the baby. Watch out for babies when your car is moving and when it's in the house just sitting there behaving itself. Especially watch out for little kids who can walk. They can turn your new RC car into a pile of plastic and wire in about 30 seconds.

Beware of cars. An RC car weighs about three pounds. Mom's car weighs about 2,000 pounds. Get the idea? Don't let the little one end up under the big one. Driving in the street is definitely not a good idea.

Beware of sewers. Guess what's small enough to fit down a storm sewer if it takes a wrong turn? That's right—the thing you saved so long for, the thing you worked so hard on to paint and decorate. In no time at all, your RC car could be gone forever if you're not careful. That's another reason not to drive in the street.

Beware of your own temper. Never drive your car AT someone. Your car is not a toy, and it can hurt someone. And your car might not end up in very good shape if you do this. If you deliberately drive at someone to tease or bother them or just to show off, don't be surprised if your car gets a good, swift kick in the rear—rear axle, that is.

Protect Your Investment

Along with these safety precautions, you should also take the time to check the mechanics of your prize RC car before and after every run. Every good mechanic knows the upkeep of a car is important to its long life. And you're the only mechanic your RC car has. It's up to you to see that everything is running properly.

Stop. Before you start to run your RC car, take a minute to go over a few key points. Follow the suggested maintenance guide that came with your car.

Look. Check the car over. Oil and lube the gears. Tighten up the drive chain. And look at the major wire connections to make sure they're clean and still connected.

Listen. The motor has its own voice. After a few runs, you'll be able to tell if something is wrong just by listening to it. If the pitch or whine is different than usual, something needs to be fixed.

Painting Your RC Car

They say don't judge a book by its cover. A fancy cover doesn't mean the book is any good. That may be true, but it still doesn't stop anyone from looking at fancy covers.

The same is true for a great paint job on your RC car. It won't make it run any better, but it sure will psych out the competition. Model painting by itself can be a great hobby, too.

Radio controlled car kits come with instructions for adding the finishing touches and painting. You can follow those in general, and then move on to applying decals and custom touches. You'll be able to spot your car on the racetrack easily if you put some of your own style into it.

Some ready-to-run models can have new bodies put on them. If you have an off-the-shelf racer and want a new look, take the car to a hobby shop for a "fitting." Many of the Lexan plastic bodies can be custom-fit, even if you have to take a few extra steps to make it work.

Getting Ready

Either way you go—kit or off-the-shelf—premium paint jobs take the right equipment. For starters, it's back to the hobby shop. You'll need to get a razor knife and package of blades if you don't have them (warning: these blades really *are* as sharp as they look). You'll probably want to start with canned spray paint in two different colors, so pick your favorites, one for the background and a brighter one for the accents.

Unlike the inside assembly, where you thought you'd never run out of pieces, the car body is usually only one piece. Lexan or other plastic bodies will require some trimming. Use your razor knife. You'll want to have an adult around to make sure you're careful.

Make all the mounting holes on the body as your kit directs. Then place the body on the car to be sure it fits. It is much easier to tell if the trimming is correct while the body is still clear.

Check that you have trimmed the body cleanly and that it does not touch any wires or rub the wheels and suspension. The paint goes on the *inside* of the shell, so make sure that no wires touch the body.

It looks pretty cool when it's clear like that, doesn't it? There's no law that says you have to paint the car, after all. You can buy extra bodies if you want a clear shell sometimes and paint a few for a new look every now and then. Compared to the insides, the body doesn't cost much at all.

Okay, you've checked the fit, and it's perfect. It's time to clean it up and get set. The inside of the body needs to be grease-free if masking tape and paint are going to stick. Start by mixing up suds in the sink, the same as you would for doing dishes. Put the body in the sink, and give it a gentle rub down with a paper towel. Be sure to wipe off the inside of the shell. Give it a rinse in cool water, and let it air dry.

The reason you want the body to air dry is to prevent any dust or fiber particles from getting on it. After it's dry, put on plastic gloves—dish gloves work fine, or use painter gloves from a hobby shop or hardware store. You don't want to leave oily fingerprints on the surface.

Masking

Now you're ready to use masking tape on the windows. A few tricks here can help you, too.

There are commercial liquid masking gels that you can use, and the experts say they are the best. You brush the gel on the underside of the body and let it dry for five to six hours. It forms a second skin on the inside of the body, sort of like a heavy flexible film coating.

When the liquid mask is dry, use a razor knife to cut away the film, and uncover the parts of the body you want to paint. It's great for tricky

A super paint job!

designs because you can move the knife to form swirls and angles that would be really hard to do with masking tape.

The only drawback is the extra time involved. The liquid mask film does add an extra few days on the painting schedule since you have to apply at least three, preferably four, coats of it and let it dry for six hours in between coats.

If you are one of those patient people who doesn't mind taking the extra time, give this stuff a try. Even if you are impatient, you should keep it in mind for when you want to do a really showy, intricate design on a second Lexan shell.

The faster masking material is tape. For your first car, tape will do the job for you. You could use either the transparent kind or a good quality masking tape, but the best tape to use is the transparent tape because it stays on better when you want it to stay on and comes off easily when you want it to come off. And it's easier to trim to the shape of the area you want to cover.

After you have washed the car body, and after it is completely dry, tape off the areas of the car that you don't want to paint. Cover the window areas with the tape, overlapping the tape where you have to use more than one piece. Don't worry about being too accurate. When you're done taping off the windows, use a razor knife to cut the tape to the exact shape you want. Don't cut too deeply, or you'll scratch the Lexan. You have to work with a razor knife that is very sharp. Dull blades won't work. If you like your fingers and want to keep them, you might want to ask that adult for some help again. (See Razor Knife Safety Tips at the end of this chapter.)

Run a strip of tape along the body line on each side to mask off where the second color is to go. Try a line down the middle of the car, too. You can cut the tape to a thin stripe with a metal ruler and the razor knife. If it doesn't go on right the first time, just try it again. Getting ready to paint will take some time. You can move the tape all you want before you paint. It's a lot easier to re-tape several times than it is to repaint.

Always start to paint with the darker color first. After you spray it on, let it dry at least one full day before you pull the tape off. If you don't, you'll be pulling some of the paint off, too. For the second color, take the tape off the areas to be painted, and then spray on the second color.

Painting Tips

Even if you've never held a paint brush outside of art class, you can still give your RC car a professional paint job.

Getting an even, smooth paint job from spray paint takes a certain skill. You are lucky that the certain skill is easy to learn. The secret is to FOLLOW THE DIRECTIONS!

That may not sound like too big a secret, but you'd be really surprised at what a difference it makes. Read the instructions on the paint can, and follow them.

Temperature. Make sure the area where you are spraying is at least 70 degrees. Spray paint can be messy, and it does stink. Your parents may want you to paint in the garage or outdoors. If you have to go outside, you're at the mercy of Mother Nature. You'll have to wait until it's warm out. Do not try to paint in the cold. It just doesn't work.

You will get a nice, smooth finish only if the paint and the plastic are at least room temperature, which means at least 70 degrees. If you are painting in the house but the paint was stored in a cold garage, be sure to let the can warm up in the house a few hours before painting.

Shake, rattle, and roll. Paint separates when it stands still, and it is your job to mix it up before you start. The paint can has a ball inside it to help mix up the paint. You need to shake the can at least 100 times before you start painting. You'll be able to hear the ball hitting the sides of the can. All throughout the painting, remember "spray, spray, shake, shake." The paint separates quickly, and you will get an uneven paint job if you don't shake it up.

Light sprays. Think thin. Probably the second biggest temptation when you have a spray can in your hand is to use lots of paint. (The biggest temptation is to write your name on the wall. Resist both temptations.) Several light coats of spray paint will work better than one heavy spray that will blob and drip.

Get in the swing. Move the can of paint like a playground swing, back and forth. Move your hand evenly across the whole car surface. Start to spray before the paint touches the car and stop the spray after you have completed one full pass. This way the start and stop blotches are not on the car.

Keep your distance. Hold the can about 10 inches from the car when you spray. It may look easier to hold the can closer, but it will result in drips and blotches.

Up is right. Always keep the can right side up. It won't spray if turned too far sideways or upside down.

Constructing a Cardboard Paint Shed

Spray paint is very stinky stuff, and it can

be messy. It's also unhealthy and dangerous if you don't work in a place that has lots of air circulation. Here are a few hints for safe and clean painting.

Get a large cardboard box to use as a paint shed. Cut an opening in the side, leaving a few inches around the edge. This keeps the overspray from getting all over the room. Grocery stores have large (three feet square) corrugated boxes that work great. You can put a wire coat hanger through the sides of the box and position the car against it for easy handling.

The inside of a cardboard box is dark. Keeping the spray paint in also means keeping the light out, and that can be trouble. Here is a simple solution to make it easier to see what you are doing. Before you start painting, cut a square out from the top of the box, and cover the hole with clear plastic wrap. Tape the plastic wrap securely at the edges. You'll have an instant skylight for your paint shed!

To air out the house *after* you're done working, open the windows, and use a room fan. You don't want a fan running while you are spraying for two reasons. The spray paint would go all over, and dust would get into your fresh paint.

Razor Knife Safety Tips

Work with an adult. Concentrate on the job you are doing. Don't be distracted. Hold the knife like a pencil. This will give you the best control. Watch where you put your other hand.

The hand that does the holding is the one likely to get cut. Hold from above and behind the knife. Use even, light pressure when you are cutting. If you have to press hard, chances are you need a new blade. For straight cuts, use a metal ruler as a guide.

Don't throw old blades in the trash without wrapping the cutting edge with tape. An even better idea is to keep them separate in the blade box and throw them away all at once in the protective box. Store the knife somewhere where younger brothers and sisters can't reach it.

Driving to Win

"Hey, the car doesn't make all that much difference," an expert driver says at the racetrack. "The car makes some, only some, of the difference. The rest—I'd say 80 percent of it—is the driver. You give me any good car to race, and I'll do better than the other drivers."

Practice Makes Perfect

That's both good news and bad news for the beginner. You should feel better because your first car probably isn't going to be the absolute best car around. It's your driving that will make the difference. But you probably don't feel all that good about it, because after all you're just a beginning driver.

No problem. Here's the rest of the good news. Racing is a sport of the young. A lot of people around the racetrack think kids are better drivers because they can react faster than older people can. Beginning drivers have another advantage. The same eye-hand coordination needed to play video games is needed to drive radio controlled cars. Most young, beginning drivers are familiar with the joy sticks of video games and have trained themselves to react quickly before they even begin racing.

Whoa! Wait up. You can't just walk out the door and win races from the beginning. All this talk was just to give you a little confidence. You can be a winner, sure. But first you have to practice.

Driving Drills

Start slow. It might sound boring, but it's true. It will be a big temptation to just open up the speed control and see what it can do. Save that for later, though, when you know what makes it turn which way and when.

Here are some general tips. Always practice in an open area, such as an empty school parking lot or an empty ball field. Driveways and backyards can be turned into practice areas, too. Just about anywhere you don't have to compete with full-size cars or a bunch of people will work. Stay away from puddles, though. Electricity and water don't mix, remember? Streets, like we said before, are not the place to drive.

Draw your temporary tracks with chalk, which will wash away and not damage anything. If you're

Thrills and chills at the track!

practicing on dirt, trace the track with a stick, or mark it off with empty aluminum cans. The cans are light enough to bounce out of the way when (not if!) your car hits them.

For more advanced track building, try the hardware store. Buy a length of dryer venting plastic coil and a dozen gutter spikes. That's the flexible tube that runs the hot air outside from the back of a clothes dryer. Secure it to the ground with some gutter spikes, which are the long, light nails used for nailing in gutters. This is perfect for forming the curves and turns of a real dirt track. This kind of track, however, is not very temporary. You'd better stick to your own property—or where you have permission—if you build one of these.

Here are few practice drills to get you started.

The basic oval. Start with an oval track to master a basic turn. Try for control, and keep the speed low. Notice how the controls are backward when the car is driving toward you? That's the tricky part. Now, turn the car around, and try it in the other direction without moving from where you are.

Figure eight. After you're comfortable with the oval, draw a large number eight on the ground, and try to maneuver it. It's a little bit harder than just driving in a straight line, isn't it?

Drag racing. A form of the sport all by itself, drag racing is a straight sprint, line to line. There are no turns and no curves. Draw a starting line, and pace off about 100 feet (that's about 35 giant steps) to the finish line. Make sure your car has plenty of room to slow down after it crosses the finish line. Now you can try that speed. Open up the speed controls, and let it rip.

This is a fun game to play with other cars, too. You can also do this for neighborhood racing. It's probably the safest type of racing for the cars—that is, if your friends can drive straight at high speeds. But it's not as easy as it sounds, as you'll see.

Slalom. Set up 10 empty pop cans in a row about two feet apart. Stand to the side. Start the car at one end of the line, and weave the car around each can. Don't go fast, just try not to hit the cans. When you can get through it without hitting anything, walk to the head of the line, and try it again. Since you are looking at it from a different angle, it will be a completely different drive. Learn how to control your car from all points around the track.

Jumping. Jumping—or, as the pros call it, ramping—is one of the more awesome driving skills. (This is for dirt trackers only. Keep your clean cars at the oval-racing level.) Take a smooth board and two bricks. Lean the board against the bricks so the drop to the ground is no more than 12 inches. Accelerate up to the jump, and let off the juice right before you fly. You'll shoot long and low, just the style you're looking for to get the farthest the fastest. When you're racing, you don't want to waste time in the air.

Strategy

One driver will tell you that you have to accelerate into a curve to get the best speed around it. That results in a "power slide," which is seen in motorcycle races quite a bit.

Another driver will tell you to save all that muscle. They say that the key to cornering is control. And finesse, not muscle, is the key to winning.

Who's right? They both are. Either strategy

will work, but you have to be comfortable with the strategy you choose. Try it both ways. Drive your car full speed into the corner, and turn it tight. Let the momentum take it through. You'll have less control, but with the right timing on the turn, your car will slide through it just fine. The advantage here is that you'll save wear and tear on your car's gears.

For controlled driving, ease up on the speed as you approach the corner, and don't give it full throttle until you're clear of the turn. You may look like you're losing ground to another car, but wait! What's that? The car that did a power slide and burned past you is now turned over on its back, wheels spinning in the air. The advantage here is that you'll save time in the long run on flips and crashes.

So, what is the best way? The way that works for you.

A Day at the Races

Jay wasn't too sure this race stuff was for him. After all, he thought, the guys here look like they have an edge. That car over there looks like it cost at least a zillion times what Jay's car cost.

This was the first time Jay and his mom had come to the indoor off-road track. No doubt about it, Jay was more than a bit scared.

The car Jay was going to race was his pride. It cost him every penny he'd earned during the past six months. Even then his mom had to lend him some money to make up the difference. She didn't seem to mind, though. Jay remembered how she drove him over to the hobby shop whenever he needed a new part or had a really tough question. Since his dad moved out of state last year, his mom really tried to help with all the things Jay was interested in.

Going into the track, Jay registered at the desk and paid his entry fee.

"What are you racing today?" the man at the desk asked Jay.

"Uh, I'm racing my car," said Jay, immediately knowing that was the dumbest answer in the world.

"Well, you're in the right place for that!" the man shouted and then laughed. "Is this your first race?"

Jay nodded.

"Welcome to the Dirt Trackers Raceway, then. What's your name?"

"Jason Thomas," Jay said. "My friends call me Jay."

"Well, Jay, my name's Sam. And I own all this dirt. I'm the race director, too. Now, let's take a look at that car."

Jay held up his RC car for inspection.

"Did you build this yourself?" Sam asked.

Jay nodded. "Well, my mom helped me with the decals and painting a little. And Steve at the hobby shop helped with the servo wiring and suspension. But mostly, yeah, I built it."

Jay felt good about having built his car, and he felt good talking about it. It's a pretty big project to build an RC car, and he'd been able to do most of it by himself. And Jay had to admit that his RC car looked pretty cool.

Sam agreed. "I see a lot of first time racers, Jay, and you've done a fine job on this car. Let's look inside."

Jay popped off the car body, exposing the intricate wiring and suspension system.

"When I asked what you're racing today, Jay, I wanted to know what class you're racing in," Sam explained. "You'll be in the factory stock novice class, where the two-wheel and four-wheel drive vehicles race together. This is just for beginners—the entry-level racer—like yourself, so don't worry about competing against more advanced drivers.

"Your car fits the requirements for the class. It has all the parts that came from the factory, and you haven't modified it in any way."

Sam put the body back on, and put the car on a scale.

"Since it's a two-wheel drive car, it has to weigh at least three pounds, four ounces, which it does." Sam smiled, handing the car back to Jay. "If it was four-wheel drive, we'd require it to weigh at least three and half pounds. That's just to make it all even and fair in the races. Your car is fine, Jay. You should have a good race today."

Jay turned to leave.

"Whoa, Jay. We're not through checking in yet," Sam said, calling him back to the registration desk. "What's your frequency?"

"It's 5.7," Jay answered, hoping that no one else had registered that frequency for his race. He hadn't brought the extra crystals that a racer needs in case someone already has that frequency in your race.

But it was okay today. No one else had that frequency.

Sam smiled and said, "Okay, Jay, you'll be number

five today. Place this number on the front windshield. Grab a spot over there, and get ready. Listen up for the announcements."

Entering the track, Jay could smell the moist dirt. It was weird to be inside and have it smell just like outside on a hot day after a rain.

Jay and his mom went over to the side wall. A narrow workbench ran the whole length of the room against the wall. Men and boys sat together, hunched over their cars, concentrating on last minute details.

"Hey, Mom," Jay whispered. "Look at that."

It was a wooden toolbox that doubled as a car carrying case. The man looked up and smiled as Jay and his mom walked past.

"What a great idea," Jay's mom said to the man, pointing to the box.

"Yeah," the man said. "I call this my traveling garage. I built it myself. It holds absolutely everything I need to work on my car, and it has it all in one place. It's heavy, but it isn't all that big. It's really handy when you have to do some repair work on the spot. It's a safe way to carry the *Flaming Fortune*. That's my car. It moves like fire, and it cost a fortune!"

The man laughed, and Jay smiled.

"My name's Bud," the man said. "You two must be new here."

"We are," said Jay's mom. "My name is Mary Ann. This is Jason, my son. We're a bit lost. Can we sit just anywhere along this wall? We didn't bring any tools or anything."

"You don't have any tools? You better sit right down here, then," Bud winked at Jay. "You're not expecting anything to break, now, are you?"

"No, sir, I mean, the car is pretty new." Jay couldn't quite understand why Bud looked so amused by his not bringing any tools with him.

"Don't you worry about it, son," Bud said. "You can borrow any tools you need from the traveling garage. But wait now. Here come the announcements."

"Welcome, racers and fans, to Dirt Trackers International Speedway!"

Jay recognized Sam's voice on the loudspeaker and asked Bud why the racers were all laughing so loudly at his welcoming words.

"International Speedway is a little joke," Bud explained. "Some of the guys take this racing so seriously that they think this is the real thing. You know what, Jay?"

"What?"

"It is the real thing!"

Bud laughed again. He was having a wonderful time explaining the inside story to Jay. Jay had heard that one of the best parts of radio controlled racing was the good time you can have with other people who enjoy the same things that you do.

Bud and Jay listened to the rest of the announcements, and then they went over to the race board to see when Jay's race was scheduled.

"You'll be first in your class," Bud said. "We race with three qualifying heats here, so you'll

55

have three runs. The racers with the best average times will go into the finals. Do you understand about corner marshalling?" Bud asked Jay.

"A little, but not very much," Jay admitted.

"Well, it's something that all racers have to do here. Corner marshalling really helps everyone work together, even though we are competing against each other," Bud said.

"At this track," Bud continued, "the guys who have completed their race stand at the edges of the track, ready to run onto the course to turn over flipped cars or pull a racer back from the wall. And remember, Jay. You can't use reverse in a race. Doing that will get you disqualified."

Jay nodded. He knew from practicing that a car in reverse was much harder to control than one going forward.

"Let's get up there on the control platform for a good look at the course," Bud said. "You'll get a good picture of what you should do in the race. And then when it's your turn to race, just take your time. You don't want to wreck the car before the finals. Just drive slow and steady, especially the first lap or two, to get an idea of where the curves, potholes, and bumps are."

Bud and Jay climbed up to the platform overlooking the course. Lining the edge of the track was a four-foot high wooden wall. The inside lanes were marked by six-inch round, plastic plumber's pipes that were held in the dirt with long spikes.

"The course is 280 feet long this week," Bud

told Jay. "The plastic pipe lets Sam rearrange the track each week."

From the starting line, the course ran 10 feet straight away and then banked left, up three feet into a wide first curve. The curve formed a chute down a hill into a narrowing turn. The soft pipe curved sharply to the right and then back to the left in almost a *Z* shape.

A straight, four-foot approach to a one-foot jump followed. Another three feet was clear for landing, with a high banking curve following to the left again. The sharp, hairpin turn back to the right was sure to test even the most careful driver's skills.

"You watch that beginning straightaway, Jay," Bud said. "You'll want to start off real fast, but just hold back. That first curve is wide, but it goes into a narrow lane. Keep it slow."

Sam's voice came over the loud speaker again.

"We'll be running factory stock one, now. Factory stock one. Racers to the platform, please. Factory stock one."

"Are you all ready to go, Jay?" his mom asked

"I'm as ready as I'll ever be," Jay said nervously.

"Go get 'em!" Jay's mom yelled from the side lines.

The four cars lined up at the chalked line on the dirt. Jay stood in the control platform with three other boys, each one looking just as nervous as Jay felt. All of a sudden, one car took off, turned sideways, and hit the wall. Jay saw driver wince with embarrassment.

"That was a false start," Sam said on the speaker. "Corner marshall, get the car please. Get the car."

It didn't sound like it was any big deal to Sam. It must happen all the time, Jay thought.

"Drivers, get ready," Sam said.

Bang!

It sounded like a cap gun, and before the sound died in the air, four RC racers whined off the starting line toward the first curve. Over the cry of the motors, Jay could hear Sam announcing the race.

"We have number 12 clearing the line first. And then we have Numbers 5, 2 and 7."

Jay kept his eyes on his car, trying to remember Bud's advice.

Through the first curve, Jay's car performed perfectly. It hugged the inside lane, bursting with speed just as it cleared the turn.

"Number 5 takes the early lead, with 12 holding steady. Numbers 2 and 7..."

Swinging back into the Z, Jay's car traveled a little too far to the left, rubbing along the side of the plastic pipe, slowing him down. Two racers passed him as he pulled out into the center of the lane as he approached the straightaway to the jump.

Crash!

The fourth racer whacked Jay's car from behind, sending it flipping on its side. The corner marshall leaped into the course, quickly turning

Jay's car back over.

"Twelve with one done, and 7 takes a circle. . ."

Jay took his eyes off his car and watched the other two racers finish their first lap. I'm not even halfway yet, he thought. What a rotten break!

Jay looked back and saw the car that had hit him had already cleared the jump. That's what I get for worrying about the other guy, Jay thought. I better get going.

He started up and took the jump like a pro, hitting it with just the right burst of speed to get a long, low clearance. I didn't waste any time there, Jay thought.

The corner marshals were busy at the Z curve again, this time with the other two racers who were almost a full lap ahead of Jay. It was their turn to crash, and one car lost a wheel. The corner marshall took it to the side. A disappointed driver left the control platform to get his broken car. This race was over for him.

Jay tried not to notice what was happening to the other drivers. Instead, he concentrated on his car, driving his race, and just doing his best.

Four laps around, Jay was getting the feel of the course. My speed is definitely improving, he thought. I can take this corner faster.

He pressed the speed control and steered clearly around the turn. The back of the car bounced in protest, and the motor whined in objection. It met the challenge, though, as it approached the leading car.

Jay swung wide to avoid another smash up, and tried to pass on the outside. The other car swung wide, blocking his way, and Jay saw he was going to have to be more shrewd in his driving strategy.

Easing back on the speed, Jay dropped behind just a bit until the cars were on the front straightaway. Whoosh! Jay hit the juice, sending dust into the air as his car blazed past the others.

I got him! Jay thought. He's just poking along back there. Oh, no, the high banked turn! I can't control it!

Shooting into the turn, Jay's car went up the slope and headed for the wall. Jay braced himself for the collision, as though he were really in the car. He pushed against the steering control as hard as he could, but he was definitely losing it. A screeching sound filled the air as Jay's car scratched along the wall. It bounced once and flipped, sliding down the embankment. The corner marshall pounced into action like a cat on a mouse, grabbing the wounded car before it finished its slide. It was right side up and ready to roll all within the blink of an eye.

"Time warning, gentlemen, time warning," announced Sam.

Still shaken, Jay drove slowly through the course one more time. He passed the other two cars in a pile-up at the jump, missing them by at least a hundredth of an inch. Finishing his last lap, he realized how fast his heart was beating. Then the race was over.

"All right, Jason!" His mom and Bud were yelling as Jay came off the control platform. "You did it!"

"I won?"

"Won?" Bud laughed. "No, you didn't win. You did it. You ran a great race. Look at that car of yours. Wow, did it take a beating! Do you want to borrow those tools now?"

"Jason, you were fabulous," his mom continued. "You raced. You finished. And you did a great job. I'm very proud of you!"

Jay smiled. No, he didn't take the checkered flag, and maybe it would be a long time before he did. But looking at his mom and his new friend, it was hard to imagine how he could feel any more like a winner than he did right then.

About the Author

C. M. Gynn is a newspaper reporter and free-lance writer in Columbus, Ohio, where she lives with her husband and ten-year-old son. When she was a teen-ager, she learned a lot about cars by helping restore a 1961 Ford Thunderbird. This knowledge of cars came in handy when she got her own car—a 1959 English sports car that needed a tuneup each time she filled the gas tank!

"It's important for young people to learn the basics of mechanics and fixing things," she says. "Hobbies like RC cars not only let you have fun, but they teach you plenty about how the world runs."